My First Animal Library

Sloths

by Mari Schuh

Ideas for Parents and Teachers

Bullfrog Books let children practice reading informational text at the earliest reading levels. Repetition, familiar words, and photo labels support early readers.

Before Reading

• Discuss the cover photo. What does it tell them?

• Look at the picture glossary together. Read and discuss the words.

Read the Book

• "Walk" through the book and look at the photos. Let the child ask questions. Point out the photo labels.

• Read the book to the child, or have him or her read independently.

After Reading

• Prompt the child to think more. Ask: Have you ever seen a sloth? Can you be as slow and still as a sloth?

Dedicated to my lazy rabbit Kindle —MS

Bullfrog Books are published by Jump!
5357 Penn Avenue South
Minneapolis, MN 55419
www.jumplibrary.com

Library of Congress Cataloging-in-Publication Data
Schuh, Mari C., 1975- author.
Sloths / by Mari Schuh.
    pages cm.—(My first animal library)
  Summary: "This photo-illustrated book for early readers describes a lazy day in the life of a sloth in the rain forest"—Provided by publisher.
  Audience: Ages 5-8.
  Audience: K to grade 3.
  Includes bibliographical references and index.
  ISBN 978-1-62031-112-7 (hardcover)
  ISBN 978-1-62496-179-3 (ebook)
1. Sloths—Juvenile literature. I. Title.
QL737.E2S38 2015
599.3'13—dc23
                                2013044264

Editor: Wendy Dieker
Series Designer: Ellen Huber
Book Designer: Lindaanne Donohoe
Photo Researcher: Kurtis Kinneman

Photo Credits: All photos by Shutterstock except: Corbis, 18, 18–19, 22; SuperStock, 5, 8–9, 10–11, 16

Printed in the United States of America at Corporate Graphics, North Mankato, Minnesota.
6-2014
10 9 8 7 6 5 4 3 2 1

Table of Contents

Life Upside Down

The sun rises.

A sloth sleeps upside down.

He hangs in a tree.

He lives alone
in the rain forest.

His claws are
like hooks.

He holds on tight.

The sloth is hard to see.
Algae live in his hair.
The tiny plants make
his hair green.

algae

Eagles look for him.

12

But they can't find him.

Shh! He is still.

He is safe.

13

The sun sets.

It is night.

The sloth wakes up.

He is slow.

He slowly eats leaves.

dew

He sips dew.

Splash!
The sloth swims in a river.
Look! He finds a new tree.
Up he goes.

A new day is here.
He tucks in his head.
It's time to sleep.

Parts of a Sloth

claws
Long, curved claws grab tree branches.

hair
Sloths are covered with long, shaggy hair.

legs
Long, strong legs help sloths hang from trees.

Picture Glossary

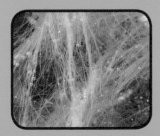

algae
Tiny plants without roots or stems that grow in wet places.

eagle
A big, strong bird that hunts during the day.

dew
Small drops of water that form on leaves and plants during the night.

rain forest
A thick area of trees where a lot of rain falls.

Index

To Learn More

Learning more is as easy as 1, 2, 3.

1) Go to www.factsurfer.com

2) Enter "sloths" into the search box.

3) Click the "Surf" button to see a list of websites.

With factsurfer.com, finding more information is just a click away.